Festival Flourish
for manuals

Kevin
Mayhew

We hope you enjoy the music in *Festival Flourish for Manuals*.
Further copies of this and our many other books are available
from your local music shop or Christian bookshop.

In case of difficulty, please contact the publisher direct by writing to:

The Sales Department
KEVIN MAYHEW LTD
Rattlesden
Bury St Edmunds
Suffolk IP30 0SZ

Phone 01449 737978
Fax 01449 737834

Please ask for our complete catalogue of outstanding Church Music.

Front Cover: *The Expulsion of the Devils from Arezzo* 1296 - 67
by Bondone Giotto (*c.* 1266 - 1337).
Courtesy of the San Francesco, Upper Church, Assissi /
Bridgeman Art Library, London.
Reproduced by kind permission.

Cover designed by Graham Johnstone and Jaquetta Sergeant.

First published in Great Britain in 1997 by Kevin Mayhew Ltd.

© Copyright 1997 Kevin Mayhew Ltd.

ISBN 1 84003 059 3
ISMN M 57004 117 6
Catalogue No: 1400150

0 1 2 3 4 5 6 7 8 9

Music Editor: Nicola Greengrass
Music setting by Vernon Turner

Printed and bound in Great Britain

Contents

About the Composers

Malcolm Archer (*b*.1952) is Organist and Master of the Choristers at Wells Cathedral. He is conductor of Wells Oratorio Society and the City of Bristol Choir, in addition to his work as a composer and recitalist.

Rosalie Bonighton (*b*.1946) is a recitalist, teacher and composer with a special interest in writing music for new liturgical needs.

Simon Clark (*b*.1975) has studied composition with many prominent English composers, including Howard Blake and Michael Finnissy. He is active in Sussex musical circles and takes a keen interest in the musical life of St Mary the Virgin Church, Hartfield.

Adrian Vernon Fish (*b*.1956) studied composition with Alan Ridout and Herbert Howells. His output is considerable, ranging from symphonies and organ music to cantatas and cabaret songs.

Andrew Fletcher (*b*.1950) was Organ Scholar at Keble College, Oxford. In addition to his work as a teacher, accompaniest and choir trainer, he is a prolific composer, has released several critically acclaimed recordings, and regularly tours worldwide as an organ recitalist.

Andrew Gant (*b*.1963) is Director of Music in Chapel at Selwyn College, Cambridge, and Organist and Master of the Choir at The Royal Military Chapel (The Guards Chapel), Wellington Barracks, London.

Colin Hand (*b*.1929) is a composer of choral, orchestral and chamber music for both professional and amateur players. He spent many years as a teacher, lecturer and examiner.

Richard Lloyd (*b*.1933) was Assistant Organist of Salisbury Cathedral and successively Organist of Hereford and Durham Cathedrals. He now divides his time between examining and composing.

John Marsh (*b*.1939) formerly Organist and Director of Music at St Mary Redcliffe Church, Bristol, is now a member of the music staff at Clifton College, Bristol.

Colin Mawby (*b*.1936) composes in many forms. He was previously Choral Director at Radio Telefís Éireann, the national broadcasting authority in the Republic of Ireland, and Master of the Music at Westminster Cathedral. He was recently appointed Conductor of the National Chamber Choir of Ireland, which is Ireland's only full-time, professional choir.

Malcolm McKelvey (*b*.1926) was Organ Scholar at St Peter's College, Oxford. He was Director of Music at Christ's Hospital in Horsham, Sussex (the Bluecoat School), for 23 years prior to his retirement in 1985.

Andrew Moore (*b*.1954) is a Benedictine priest. He studied at the Royal Academy of Music and at Cambridge University.

Philip Moore (*b*.1943) is Organist and Master of the Music at York Minster.

June Nixon is Organist and Director of the Choir at St Paul's Cathedral, Melbourne, Australia. She also teaches at the Melbourne University School of Music.

James Patten (*b*.1936) is a composer and conductor who has held a variety of lecturing posts at Universities and Colleges, including Professor of Composition at Trinity College of Music.

Richard Proulx (*b*.1937) is a composer, conductor and organist. He was Music Director at the Cathedral of the Holy Name in Chicago for fourteen years. His ensemble 'The Cathedral Singers' is well known for its series of recordings of both early music and original works.

Noel Rawsthorne (*b*.1929) was Organist of Liverpool Cathedral for twenty-five years and City Organist and Artistic Director at St George's Hall, Liverpool. He was also Senior Lecturer in Music at St Katherine's College, Liverpool, until his retirement in 1993. In 1994 he was awarded an honorary degree of Doctor of Music by the University of Liverpool.

Betty Roe (*b*.1930) studied at the Royal Academy of Music and later with Lennox Berkeley. She composes in many forms from solo songs to operas.

Martin Setchell (*b*.1949) is an English-born and trained musician, choral conductor and organ recitalist now working in New Zealand, where he is a Senior Lecturer in Music at the University of Canterbury in Christchurch and organist at the Christchurch Town Hall.

Quentin Thomas (*b*.1972) is a member of the teaching staff at the Oratory School, Woodcote, Berkshire. He is also active as a conductor, performer and composer.

Stanley Vann (*b*.1910) was successively Organist at Chelmsford and Peterborough Cathedrals.

Alan Viner (*b*.1951) was formerly Director of Music at the Priory Boys' Grammar School, Shrewsbury, and the Wakeman School, Shrewsbury. He now devotes his time to private teaching, composing and accompanying.

Norman Warren (*b*.1934) is Archdeacon of Rochester. He is well-known as a composer of hymns, and was a member of the music committee for 'Hymns for Today's Church'.

FESTAL TRUMPETS

Noel Rawsthorne

PROMENADE

June Nixon

AN ENGLISH DANCE

Simon Clark

With movement, but not too fast

a tempo

ten.

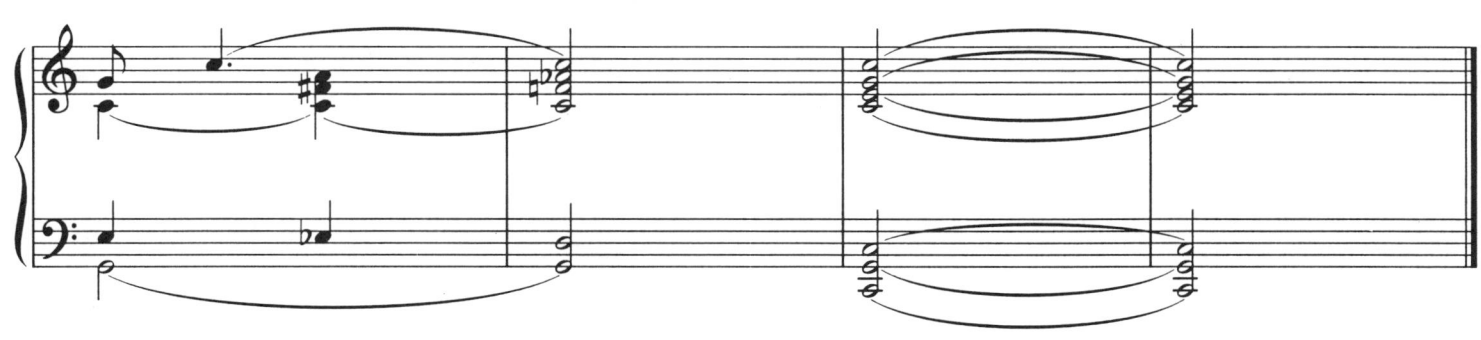

JOYFUL PROCESSIONAL

Andrew Gant

SONG OF JOY

Norman Warren

BERECHIAH'S BAGATELLE

Richard Lloyd

LAETENTUR COELI

Philip Moore

TOCCATINO

Malcolm McKelvey

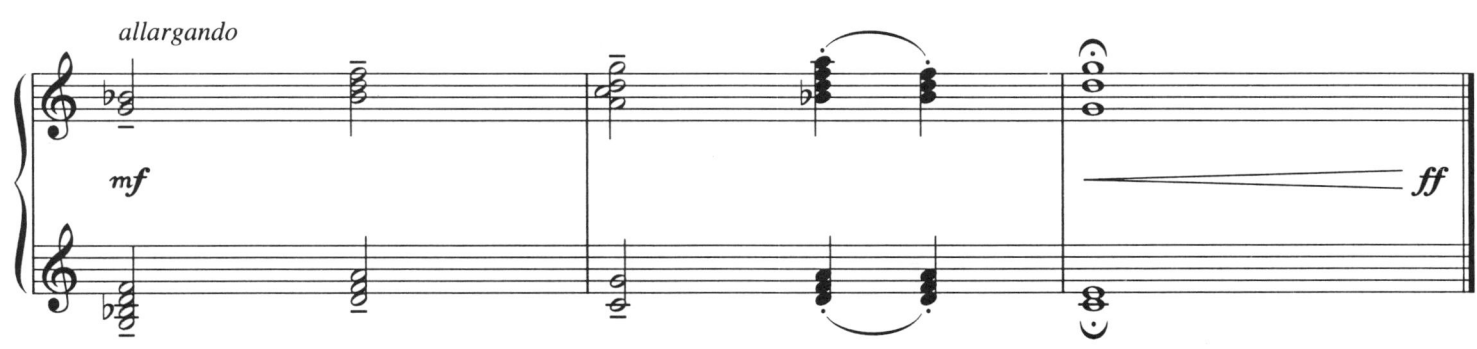

A PEAL OF JOY

Colin Mawby

SEBASTIAN'S FLIGHT

Andrew Fletcher

With apologies to S.S. Wesley's 'Choral Song'

MARZIALE

Quentin Thomas

OUR LADY'S MORNING SONG

Stanley Vann

* Delicate but bright registration

TOCCATINA FOR A SPRING MORNING

Colin Hand

38

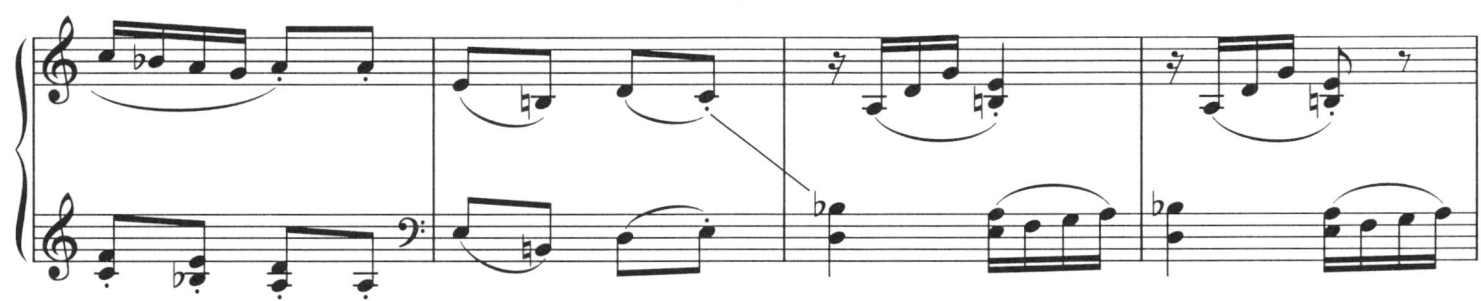

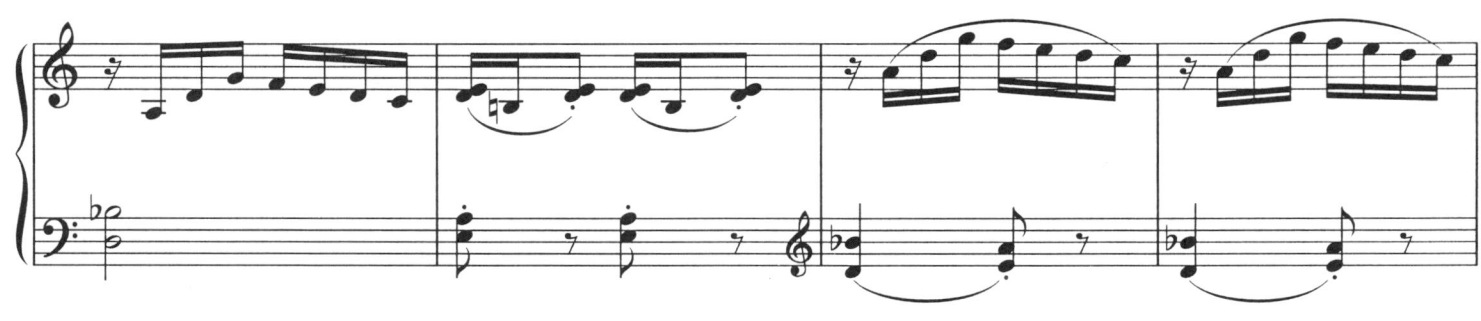

JOYFUL PROCESSION

James Patten

43

LAUDAMUS TE

Adrian Vernon Fish

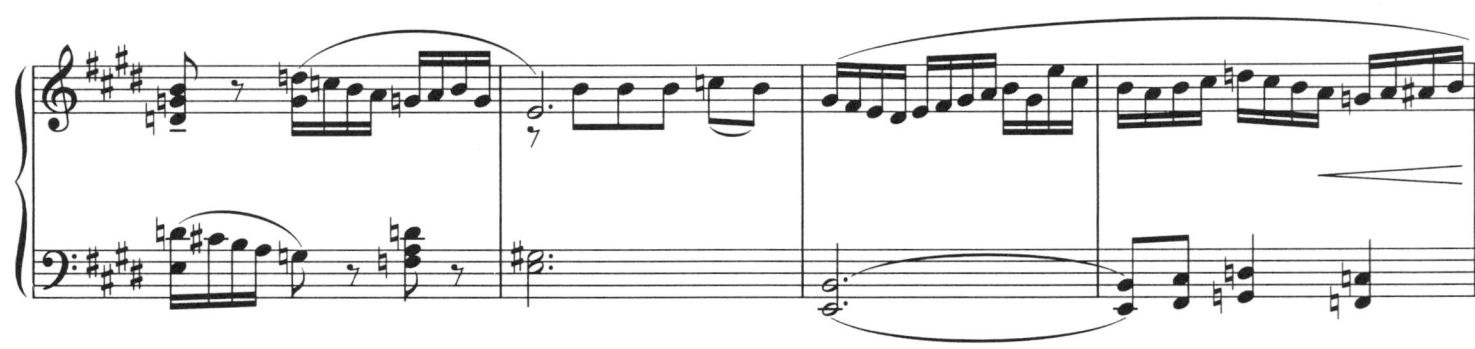

DANSE SACRÉE

Richard Proulx

For a shorter postlude, the bars between ⌐ and ¬ may be omitted.

51

PLAYFUL PROCESSIONAL

Martin Setchell

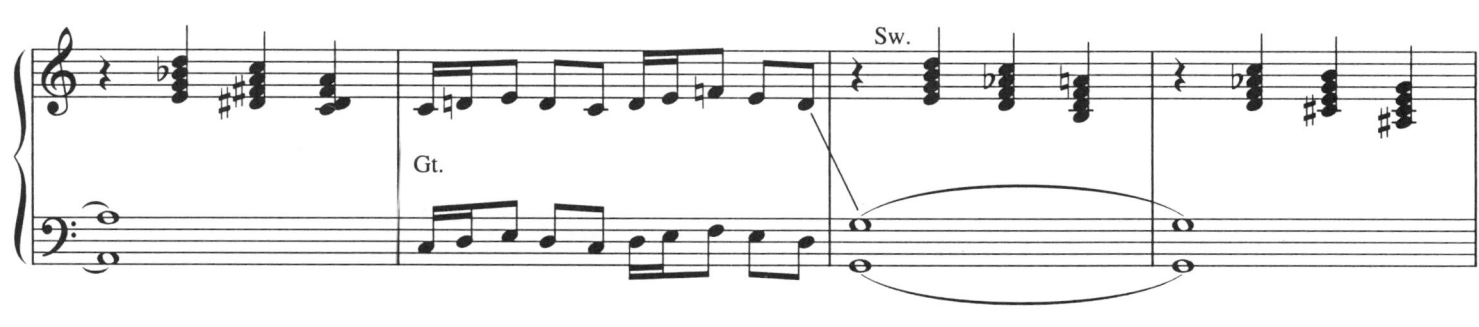

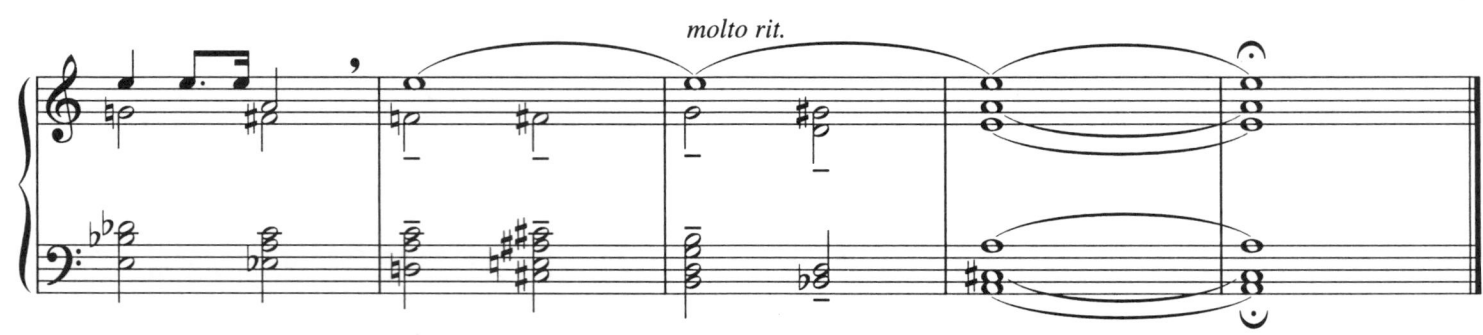

ALLEGRO SCHERZANDO

Alan Viner

* *The registration should be bright throughout.*

For an Old Puffin

IN THREES

Betty Roe

OFF-BEAT TOCCATA

Rosalie Bonighton

CAPRICE

John Marsh

RONDINO

Andrew Moore

SUN AND WIND SCHERZO

Malcolm Archer

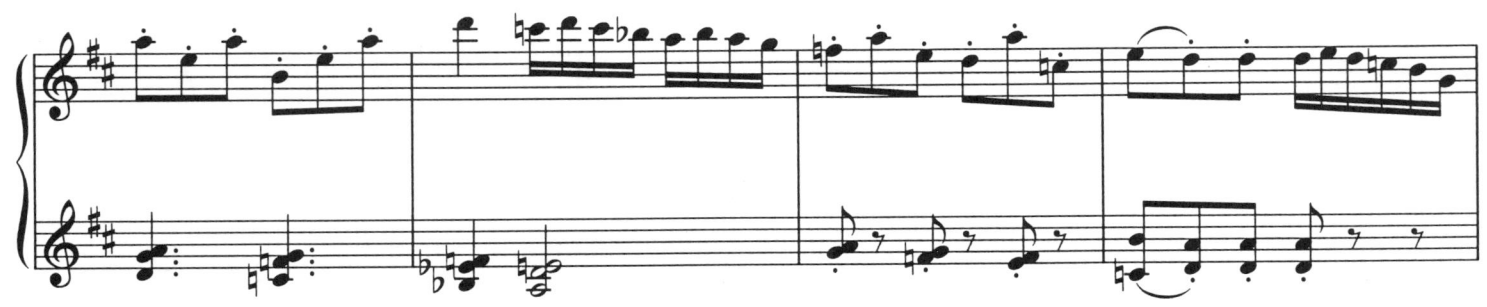